BRINGING THE BIBLE TO LIFE

Genesis, by John H. Walton, Janet Nygren, and Karen H. Jobes
(12 sessions)

Esther, by Karen H. Jobes and Janet Nygren
(8 sessions)

John, by Gary M. Burge, Karen Lee-Thorp, and Karen H. Jobes
(12 sessions)

Romans, by Douglas J. Moo, Karen Lee-Thorp, and Karen H. Jobes
(12 sessions)

Ephesians, by Klyne Snodgrass, Karen Lee-Thorp, and Karen H. Jobes
(6 sessions)

Hebrews, by George H. Guthrie, Janet Nygren, and Karen H. Jobes
(8 sessions)

BRINGING
THE
BIBLE
TO LIFE

ESTHER

God Fulfills a Promise

Karen H. Jobes
Janet Nygren
Series Editor, Karen H. Jobes

ZONDERVAN®

ZONDERVAN.com/
AUTHORTRACKER
follow your favorite authors

Bringing the Bible to Life: Esther
Copyright © 2008 by Karen H. Jobes and Janet Nygren

ISBN 978-0-310-27649-4

Interior design by Michelle Espinoza

Printed in the United States of America

08 09 10 11 12 13 14 • 23 22 21 20 19 18 17 16 15 14 13 12 11 10 9 8 7 6 5 4 3 2 1

CONTENTS

SERIES PREFACE

Have you ever been in a small-group Bible study where the leader read a passage from the Bible and then invited group members to share what the passage meant to them? God wants to speak to each person individually through the Bible, but such an approach to group study can often be a frustrating and shallow experience for both leader and participants. And while the same passage can speak to people in various ways, the meat of the Word is found in what the biblical writer intended to say about God and our relationship to him. The Bringing the Bible to Life series is for those who are ready to move from a surface reading of the Bible into a deeper understanding of God's Word.

But the Bible, though perhaps familiar, was written in ancient languages and in times quite different from our own, so most readers need a bit more help getting to a deeper understanding of its message. A study that begins and ends with what a passage "means to me" leaves the meaning of the passage unanchored and adrift in the thoughts—and perhaps the misunderstanding—of the reader. But who has time to delve into the history, language, cultures, and theology of the Bible? That's the work of biblical scholars who spend their lives researching, teaching, and writing about the ancient Scriptures. The need is to get the fruit of all that research into the hands of those in small-group Bible studies.

Zondervan's NIV Application Commentary (NIVAC) series was written to bring the best of evangelical biblical scholarship to those who want to know *both* the historical meaning of the biblical text *and* its contemporary significance. This companion series, Bringing the Bible to Life, is intended to bring that material into small-group studies in an easy-to-use format. Pastors, Christian education teachers, and small-group leaders whether in church, campus, or home settings will find these guides to be an enriching resource.

Each guide in the series provides an introduction to the biblical book that concisely summarizes the background information needed to better understand the original historical context. Six to twelve sessions per guide, each session consisting of eleven or twelve discussion questions, allow a focused study that moves beyond superficial Bible reading. Relevant excerpts from the corresponding NIVAC commentary provide easy access into additional material for those interested in going even deeper. A closing section in each session assists the group in responding to God's Word together or individually. Guidance for leading each session is included, making the task of small-group leadership more manageable for busy lives.

If you want to move from the biblical text to contemporary life on solid ground, this series has been written for you.

Karen H. Jobes, PhD
Gerald F. Hawthorne Professor of
New Testament Greek and Exegesis
Wheaton College and Graduate School

OF SPECIAL NOTE

Your experience with and understanding of the book of Esther can be deepened and enriched by referring to the volume on which it is based: *The NIV Application Commentary: Esther* by Karen H. Jobes, published by Zondervan in 1999.

INTRODUCTION

Sensuality. Brutality. Political intrigue. Family feuds. Fatal character flaws. Sounds more like a modern plot than a book in the Bible. The story of Esther is all that—and then add the fact that God isn't even mentioned! No wonder some have questioned throughout the ages whether Esther belongs in the Bible, and what sort of religious message it might have. In fact, the book of Esther has provoked controversy among scholars for centuries because it is so unlike other books of Scripture.

The author who wrote Esther was very gifted in crafting a literary work rich with irony, symbolism, humor, and complex character development. He structured the story so that its form and content mutually reinforce its message. The story intentionally draws you in to relate to its characters—characters who had ambiguous morals and who were living at a time when people weren't sure if God cared anymore. Sound familiar? Though the world has changed, people basically haven't. That's why the message of Esther is so relevant today and why it's still the centerpiece of the popular Jewish festival, Purim. None of us is perfect, and it doesn't take a scholar to know we don't live in a perfect world—in fact, it can take just one person to totally ruin our lives. Enter the villain of the story. But just when things look their most hopeless, one "chance" event suddenly changes everything. In that sense, Esther is a story that is reflected in all of history, and even points to how the seemingly insignificant life of Jesus produced a radical change in the history of the world and in millions of individual lives.

To make these connections, though, it helps to have a little background to the story. When God chose Israel to be identified as "his" people, he put them in a special place to live—but there were certain conditions. If they feared the Lord as their one and only God and obeyed the commands of his covenant, then they would receive his blessings. If they disobeyed God, then the same covenant brought a curse on them. Sounds simple enough, but over the centuries it was a constant struggle.

To make a very long story short, God was faithful to his covenant with Israel but his people were not. And so God's faithfulness to his covenant promises meant driving them out of the land as the punishment he had promised if they were unfaithful to the covenant (Deut. 4:23–31). For God must be faithful both to bless and to punish just as the covenant said he would. And so God allowed other nations to defeat his people and scatter them throughout the known world. When in 586 BC the Babylonian king Nebuchadnezzar destroyed the temple in Jerusalem — understood to be the place where God dwelled on earth — the calamity left big theological questions in their minds as to whether God would still be there for them. No temple. No Promised Land. No sacrificial system remaining. Was it all over? Was their covenant with God a thing of the past?

This national catastrophe led to a revival of sorts for some. Some of the faithful Jews got a lot stricter about abandoning their idols and following God's laws, even if it was a bit late. After about seventy years of living in Babylon, another national upheaval occurred when the Persian king Cyrus defeated the Babylonians and let exiled peoples return to their homelands. In 537 BC about fifty thousand Jews were allowed to return to Israel to rebuild Jerusalem and its temple. But most didn't want to head back. Imagine if your family settled where you live now seventy years ago. Would you really want to go back to your homeland, especially if your city was only a heap of rocks? You can understand why some chose to stay in Persia.

The book of Esther is set in Susa, one of the capital cities of Persia (modern-day Iran). It is a story about the Jews who stayed in Persia after others had gone back to Jerusalem. They still maintained their Jewish identity, but it's not hard to imagine some of their practices getting watered down or even lost. Persia was quite the multicultural place because of the mix of nations that had been conquered and resettled there throughout the centuries. We're told in the first chapter of Esther that the Persian empire extended all the way from India to Ethiopia, so all sorts of cultural habits and religions were added to the mix and tolerated by the Persians. But the Jews apparently stood out enough to get noticed.

The absence of God in the book of Esther fits in with the cultural climate of the day, which is actually similar to our setting today in societies that go about their business without regard for God. But even though God is not mentioned in the story, we get a clear sense of how he's very much alive and actively working through the details of life in ancient Persia, and that he continues to do so today. Read on to learn more from this very rich and unusual book of the Bible that we call Esther.

POWER IN THE PERSIAN COURT

Esther 1:1 – 22

War clouds were gathering on the eastern horizon as the two great superpowers of the day, Persia and Greece, faced off. In the opulent court of Xerxes, king of Persia, lavish days of banqueting were underway as Xerxes entertained the men who would lead his army against Greece. No one was paying any attention to the Jews, dispersed among the peoples of Persia, much less to a beautiful, young Jewish woman named Hadassah. The God of this scattered people was virtually unheard of and certainly not mentioned as the Persians gathered their forces. In Esther chapter 1, Xerxes flexes his power with unexpected consequences for his own family—consequences that extend into every household of the empire. This surprising episode of the age-old battle of the sexes sets into play a chain of events that demonstrates God's power to direct history for his own purposes through seemingly insignificant details. Chapter 1 also foreshadows elements of the story in the rest of the book.

XERXES' WEALTH AND POWER[1]

Read Esther 1:1 – 8.

The Persian King Xerxes, who ruled from 486 – 465 BC, is also known by the Hebrew name Ahasuerus in some English translations. Xerxes is probably the Greek transliteration of his Persian name Khshayarshan. In Hebrew his name takes the form Ahasuerus, pronounced "Ahashwerosh."

1. What's the most opulent place you've ever been? Imagine yourself in the lavish setting of a garden banquet with hangings of white and blue linen fluttering in the breeze, couches gilded with gold and silver and a beautiful mosaic pavement of colorful and costly stones. You're offered wine served in goblets of gold. What are your first impressions of King Xerxes? How do you think those attending that banquet would have viewed the king?

GOING DEEPER

The banquet held "in the third year" of Xerxes' reign (1:3) corresponds well with the great war council of 483 BC, held to plan for the Persian invasion of Greece. Xerxes was mustering the nobles, officials, military leaders, princes, and governors of the provinces in Susa to rally support for his military campaign against the Greeks. The vast expanse of the Persian empire, from modern Pakistan in the east to modern Turkey in the west, encompassed many people groups with different languages, ethnic origins, and religions. Maintaining their support and loyalty over such a diverse and far-flung empire was no small feat. During the 180 days of the council, Xerxes displayed his wealth and glory to consolidate the leaders of the many provinces of the empire under his authority and to gain their loyalty to his cause.[2]

2. By the time the book of Esther was written, the original readers would have been well aware that King Xerxes suffered a surprising defeat by the Greeks that depleted his royal wealth. How does knowing this historical fact affect your reading of the story? How does it influence your view of King Xerxes? Of the leaders of powerful nations in general?

THE COMPLEX ROLE OF A QUEEN[3]

Read Esther 1:9–12.

3. One wonders how often queens of ancient empires were commanded to display their beauty at a big party. How does Queen Vashti's response to King Xerxes threaten his power and embarrass his plans?

4. The interaction between King Xerxes and Queen Vashti presents a complex example of submission — within a marriage, to a ruler, and to a higher moral authority. Is Queen Vashti's refusal justified? Is the king's anger justified? Why or why not?

GOING DEEPER

Note that this passage is the first of many in which the author refrains from making any moral or ethical evaluation. He does not fault the king for drinking, nor does he commend or condemn Vashti for refusing to appear at the king's command. The ethical and moral ambiguity of the characters is an important element in the story and is particularly appropriate to its meaning and application, for divine providence works through human behavior that flows from even the most ambiguous and confused of motives.[4]

5. How does Queen Vashti's interaction with King Xerxes set the stage for Esther, who will become the next queen?

POWER IN THE COURT[5]

Read Esther 1:13–22.

6. It's certainly appropriate for leaders to surround themselves with advisers—in fact, quite a few Scriptures would support that, such as Proverbs 11:14: "For lack of guidance a nation falls, but victory is won through many advisers." Do King Xerxes' advisers strike you as wise men? Why or why not? What might be motivating their advice?

7. How does King Xerxes' reliance on his advisers affect your view of his character as a leader?

8. Remember that King Xerxes' kingdom includes 127 provinces stretching from India to Cush (Est. 1:1). His edict travels to all of them, in their own languages (1:22). How do you think the king's royal decree will ultimately affect his reputation?

GOING DEEPER The author is cynical about the powers of this world. Although the Persian king and his officials hold such power, with this episode the author questions if they are really ever in control. Is their word truly irrevocable? In his description of how Vashti's defiance was handled, the author is mocking the inner weakness of the outwardly most powerful empire of that time.[6]

9. The advisers are quite matter-of-fact about the respect women will have for their husbands once they hear the proclamation. How does the respect commanded in the king's royal decree (1:20) differ from the respect commanded in Ephesians 5:21 – 33? Which approach is more effective? Why?

10. How would your life and morals as a Jew, living anywhere in the known world (i.e., the Persian empire), have been affected by this powerful, but morally ambiguous king? (Keep this in mind for later edicts issued by King Xerxes as well.)

11. Read Psalm 2 and Mark 10:42–45. How is the kingdom of Xerxes different from the kingdom of God? What would you think is God's view of leaders such as King Xerxes?

GOING DEEPER

The King of kings condemns the type of leadership exemplified in Xerxes' court and by the countless kings, presidents, and world leaders since. As a backdrop for the story of the salvation of God's people in the Persian period, the author of the book of Esther provides an example of the type of worldly leadership Jesus condemned: The rulers of the Gentiles were indeed lording it over the people of their empire and exercising their authority to demand a respect that they feared would not otherwise be forthcoming. In stark contrast, the leadership of Jesus was motivated not by his own personal fears and anxieties, but by the needs of those he governs as King of the universe.[7]

12. Several seemingly insignificant actions or decisions have far-reaching effects in this chapter. Identify and reflect on such moments in your own life. How does God use these moments to accomplish greater purposes in your life and in his kingdom?

RESPONDING TO GOD'S WORD

Jesus transformed our understanding of power when the King of all kings came to earth as a humble baby. Just imagine! God the Creator took on the form of a creature himself, but arrived virtually unnoticed except by a handful of shepherds. A seemingly insignificant event transformed human history.

IN YOUR GROUP OR ON YOUR OWN:

Read aloud through the words to the Christmas hymn, "Once in Royal David's City," by Cecil Frances Alexander and Henry John Gauntlett, or, if you are so inclined, you can sing it, but think about the words as you do. Take some time as a group to discuss or reflect upon what this hymn implies, then pray and thank God for his humble means of unleashing the power of his redeeming love.

ONCE IN ROYAL DAVID'S CITY[8]

Once in royal David's city stood a lowly cattle shed,
Where a mother laid her baby in a manger for his bed;
Mary was that mother mild, Jesus Christ, her little child.

He came down to earth from heaven, who is God and Lord of all,
And his shelter was a stable, and his cradle was a stall.
With the poor and mean and lowly, lived on earth our Savior holy.

For he is our childhood's pattern; day by day, like us, he grew;
He was little, weak, and helpless, tears and smiles, like us he knew;
And he cares when we are sad, and he shares when we are glad.

And our eyes at last shall see him, through his own redeeming love;
For that child so dear and gentle is our Lord in heaven above;
And he leads his children on to the place where he is gone.

NOTES

1. This section is based on *The NIV Application Commentary: Esther* (hereafter referred to as *NIVAC: Esther*), by Karen H. Jobes (Zondervan, 1999), 57–65.
2. Jobes, 60.
3. This section is based on *NIVAC: Esther*, 66–76.
4. Jobes, 75.
5. This section is based on *NIVAC: Esther*, 77–92.
6. Jobes, 85.
7. Jobes, 89.
8. Online May 9, 2007 at http://www.carols.org.uk/once_in_royal_davids_city.htm

WHAT'S A NICE GIRL LIKE YOU DOING IN A PLACE LIKE THIS?

Esther 2:1–18

Introducing ... Esther! Beauty queen? Bible heroine? Are the two compatible? Let's face it, we don't usually think of the winners of beauty contests as the most godly women today. But why not? What's it really like to live out your faith in secular society? Esther reminds us of the challenges, and yes, even the failures that may be involved. It's not always as black and white as we'd like it to be, is it?

ESTHER IN THE PERSIAN COURT[1]

Read Esther 2:1–18.

GOING DEEPER In the four years ... between the dethroning of Queen Vashti and the crowning of Queen Esther, King Xerxes suffered a disastrous defeat by the Greeks. Herodotus, a Greek historian, wrote that Xerxes enveloped himself in sensual overindulgence following this period of great loss.[2]

1. In Esther chapter 1, King Xerxes comes across as a powerful but morally ambiguous character. In chapter 2, he hasn't changed; one can only imagine the budget he has for the upkeep of all his women! What is the purpose of the king's orders and edicts presented in the book of Esther so far (1:19; 2:2–4)? What impact do King Xerxes' orders in chapter 2 have on the lives of his subjects?

GOING DEEPER

After spending one night in the king's bed, [a concubine] was returned to the harem of concubines, where she would spend the rest of her life in luxurious but desolate seclusion. Her life had been preempted by the king's pleasure. She could not leave the harem to marry or return to her family. The woman would not even see the king again, unless he asked for her by name. Children conceived by the king in these unions were raised to serve their father in high positions, but they were not legitimate heirs to the throne.[3]

2. Given the environment of the Persian court, what would the chances seem to be for a Jewish girl to have any voice in the affairs of the Persian nation?

3. Esther is introduced for the first time in chapter 2. How is she characterized? Who does she please? How does she accomplish this?

GOING DEEPER In Hebrew narrative the physical attributes described when a character is first introduced is of special relevance to his or her role in the story. By describing Esther's beauty, the author is aligning her with the women already mentioned in the story, beautiful Queen Vashti and the beautiful young virgins, thus creating a certain expectation of how Esther will fare in the Persian court.[4]

4. The orphaned Jewish girl somehow passes all the harem tests with flying colors, noticeably rising above other beautiful young women from every province. How has Esther assimilated Persian culture? What aspects of Esther's faith might be compromised in her obedience to the king and harem adviser (see Ex. 20:8–11; Deut. 14:3–21; 7:3–4, 6–11)? Do you think Mordecai bears any responsibility for Esther's actions? Explain.

GOING DEEPER Esther is the only person in the story with two names. [This is] the author's way of depicting Esther as a young woman trying to live in two worlds—the Jewish world in which she was raised and the opulent world of the Persian court into which she was thrust.[5]

FAITH IN REAL LIFE[6]

5. Religion is often thought of as a list of do's and don'ts that can be somewhat overbearing, but from God's perspective, true faith with obedience offers the very best way to live. What benefits of her faith might Esther be missing out on by covering up her Jewish identity? Do you think she found favor with God in her behavior in chapter 2? Why or why not? What judgments are made on Esther for her actions by the author of the book of Esther?

6. Esther won the favor of everyone who saw her, including the king (2:15–17). All the evidence points to a chance at success in the Persian court. Does this excuse Esther's compromising of her Jewish faith? Why or why not?

7. God is not mentioned once in the entire book of Esther—unique for a book of the Bible. Yet Esther is still part of the overall story of Scripture. Why is it important to keep in mind that this book is in the Bible and is about the Jewish people?

GOING DEEPER

The story is not about how, coincidentally, one group happens to win against the other through an extraordinary chain of events.... The story is not about conflict between any two hostile peoples; it is about the hostility of the world against God's people. Against all odds, in some inscrutable and mysterious way, the events of human history work to fulfill the promises of the covenant the Lord made with his people at Sinai.... While God may be good to all his creatures in general, he is in a special relationship of protection and preservation with his covenant people.[7]

8. Esther is not the only one who lived in a multicultural society. Just think of the variety of foods now available in our grocery stores, reflecting the tastes of the many cultures within our communities. In what ways does Esther's apparent assimilation with Persian culture compare with a modern-day Christian's assimilation of the culture in which he or she lives?

GOING DEEPER

The extent to which a Christian adopts the culture and society in which she or he lives is a major issue, not only for the individual, but also for the apologist and theologian.... Missionaries must think long and hard when taking the gospel to another culture, to decide what are the non-negotiables of the Christian life and what are cultural options. The issue of relating one's faith to one's culture is everpresent, yet most Christians live without thinking deeply and seriously about its implications.[8]

9. The Bible tells Christians to live differently from the rest of the world because of faith in Jesus Christ, but many of the options facing Christians today are not explicitly addressed in Scripture. What aspects of Christian living should remain distinct from the culture in which a person happens to live?

10. It's often easier to see the error of others' ways while missing it in your own life. The logs we leave floating in our eyes can distort our view of reality (see Matt. 7:4). Can you think of a time you compromised your own faith to gain the favor of others? How has God used that experience in your life? How can you act as an ambassador of Christ toward someone else who has compromised his or her faith?

GOING DEEPER

This episode from Esther's life offers great encouragement and comfort when we find ourselves in situations where every choice is an odd mix of right and wrong. Only God knows the end of our story from its beginning. We are responsible to him for living faithfully in obedience to his word in every situation as we best know how. Even if we make the "wrong" decision, whether through innocent blunder or deliberate disobedience, our God is so gracious and omnipotent that he is able to use that weak link in a chain of events that will perfect his purposes in us and through us.[9]

RESPONDING TO GOD'S WORD

IN YOUR GROUP:

What does it mean to be honest with one another about your shortcomings? How is an open environment helpful? How can it be a hindrance? Close your time by reading together the prayer of St. Francis of Assisi, printed below.[10]

ON YOUR OWN:

Spend some time confessing ways you have compromised your faith or judged others who have done so. Consider the prayer of St. Francis of Assisi:

Lord, make me an instrument of your peace,
Where there is hatred, let me sow love;
where there is injury, pardon;
where there is doubt, faith;
where there is despair, hope;
where there is darkness, light;
where there is sadness, joy;
O Divine Master, grant that I may not so much seek to be consoled as to
*   console;*
to be understood as to understand;
to be loved as to love.
For it is in giving that we receive;
it is in pardoning that we are pardoned;
and it is in dying that we are born to eternal life.

NOTES

1. This section is based on *NIVAC: Esther*, 93–103.
2. Jobes, 94.
3. Jobes, 110.
4. Jobes, 96.
5. Jobes, 97 citing Leland Ryken.
6. This section is based on *NIVAC: Esther*, 103–115.
7. Jobes, 103.
8. Jobes, 105.
9. Jobes, 114–115.
10. Online May 9, 2007 at http://www.prayerguide.org.uk/stfrancis.htm

CONFLICT IN THE COURT

Esther 2:19 – 3:15

The plot thickens. Mordecai and Haman are the classic good and bad guys. You could cut through the tension with a knife, and the original audience knows it — for it's a feud that goes way back, adding drama to the story. Is God really part of this story? As the unseen player, we begin to see how he uses ordinary, everyday circumstances to do just what he wants — even through something as random as throwing dice. That's what divine providence is all about.

CHARACTER DEVELOPMENT: MORDECAI AND HAMAN[1]

Read Esther 2:5 – 6 and 2:19 – 3:15.

GOING DEEPER

In Hebrew narrative the attributes described when a character is introduced are key to understanding his or her role in the story.[2]

1. What is the defining attribute of Mordecai (2:5–6)? What well-known Israelite shares Mordecai's family history (see 1 Sam. 9:1–2)?

GOING DEEPER

"Sitting at the gate" ... refers to holding an official position in the court. The gate entering into the walled palace complex was a large building in which legal, civil, and commercial business was transacted.[3]

2. The phone rings unexpectedly; the headlines shock us with some new development; a friend shares some alarming news. We never quite know what events might bring drastic change into our lives—even at the point when they happen. What defining action transpires at the gate, to the credit of Mordecai (2:21–23)? How does his action contrast with the advice and actions of other officials we have seen so far in Esther?

3. "After these events, King Xerxes honored _____" (3:1). In light of the verses leading up to this statement, who would you expect to receive the king's honor? Who is actually being honored?

GOING DEEPER

Given Mordecai's demonstrated loyalty to the king, promotion would have been an appropriate reward. The author places the promotion of Haman just where the original readers would have expected a report of Mordecai's reward as a benefactor of the king. Haman's introduction forms an unexpected twist when juxtaposed with Mordecai's unrewarded loyalty....

While Mordecai went unrewarded for quite some time, the man who would eventually attempt to eliminate the Jews was rising to a position in the court where he had the power to actually make good on such a threat. But had Mordecai been rewarded immediately as was custom, there would have been no opportunity for the deferred reward to become a crucial link in the deliverance of the Jews from the threat of genocide.... These unfolding events begin to show the inscrutable interplay between circumstances thrust upon us, sometimes unjustly, and those the result of our own behavior, often flawed. God's providence marvelously moves through both in his own good time.[4]

4. What is the defining attribute of Haman (3:1)? Who does Haman trace his family history back to (see 1 Sam. 15:7–8)?

5. Mordecai's and Haman's family histories are linked throughout the unfolding story of the nation of Israel. Look through the following passages to get a feel for the "bad blood" between them: Exodus 17:8–16; Deuteronomy 25:17–19; and 1 Samuel 15:1–9. What do you learn from these passages?

GOING DEEPER

Agag was the king of the Amalekites at the time Saul (also of the tribe of Benjamin) was the first king of Israel. The Amalekites were a nomadic people of the southern desert region who frequently raided Israel from the beginning of its history. This heathen nation had the dubious distinction of being the first people of the world to attack and try to destroy God's newly formed covenant nation. Because of this, God promised Moses that he would completely erase the memory of the Amalekites from under heaven and would be at war with them from generation to generation.[5]

6. Put yourself in the shoes of Mordecai and Haman. How does the historical enmity between the Jews and the Agagites add to the conflict presented between Mordecai and Haman in chapter 3?

GOING DEEPER

Over the centuries after Saul spared Agag's life, other perennial enemies of Israel were called Agagites, even though they had no ethnic relationship to the Amalekites ... Rabbinic tradition held that Haman was in fact a descendant of Agag. However, ... Haman need not have been genetically descended from the Amalekites to have earned the name Agagite.[6]

7. Mordecai refuses to kneel down before Haman and Haman is enraged (3:5). But Haman doesn't stop there. How does Haman's resulting plan against Mordecai (3:6) mirror the reactions of King Xerxes (1:12) and his advisers (1:16–20)?

8. King Xerxes has been influenced on two occasions already in the book of Esther. His advisers have manipulated him to issue edicts that serve their own purposes, convincing him at the time that they serve the king's own self-interest: first to depose Vashti, and then to search for a suitable replacement for the queen. How does Haman make use of King Xerxes' style of leadership for his own ends (3:8–9)? What is the result?

GOING DEEPER

Herodotus reports that the annual revenue of the Persian empire under Xerxes' father, Darius, was 14,560 thousand talents. This revenue was generated by receiving tribute (i.e., taxes) from the satrapies. Haman's offer to provide ten thousand talents of silver (about 300 tons) represents a substantial contribution to the royal coffers. Haman may have thrown out an exaggerated figure of ten thousand talents to sell his idea. Presumably, whatever revenue he promises will come by plundering the possessions of those killed.[7]

GOD'S PROVIDENCE[8]

9. Haman threw dice (cast the *pur*, or lot) in order to decide what day to destroy the Jews. Examine other results of the lot in Psalm 16:5–6 and Proverbs 16:33. Who determines the results of the lot? Is it a trustworthy form of decision-making?

To determine the propitious time for an attack on the Jews, Haman consults the *pur* (pl., *purim*) or lot. Archaeologists have unearthed samples of *purim*, which were clay cubes inscribed with either cuneiform characters or dots that look almost identical to modern dice. "Casting the lot" literally meant throwing the dice. But unlike their modern use, the ancient lot was used not for gambling but for divination. It was a way of asking the gods for answers to questions about the future.... The *pur* or *goral* was used also by ancient Israel to query Yahweh.[9]

10. What day is Haman's edict sent out to the Persian empire (3:12)? Amazingly enough, this is the eve of a very special day for the Jews (see Lev. 23:5). What significance might this "coincidence" have for the Jews?

To the Jewish reader, Haman's casting of the *pur* and the resulting edict of death on Passover eve would be profoundly ironic, suggesting the critical question: "Would God still deliver his people, now in exile in Persia, even though they had violated the very covenant in which he promised protection?" In other words, the knowledgeable reader would be asking whether the covenant with Yahweh, celebrated by Passover, was still in effect for the Jews of Persia.[10]

11. Jeremiah the prophet cried out to God, "You are always righteous, Lord, when I bring a case before you. Yet I would speak with you about your justice: Why does the way of the wicked prosper? Why do all the faithless live at ease?" (Jer. 12:1). How does the bewilderment of Susa (Est. 3:15) echo Jeremiah's questioning of God? Why would faith and trust in God's providence be of particular importance for Mordecai at this time?

12. Can you think of a time in your own life when the outcome of a difficult, or even unjust situation, wasn't clear? How did you respond? What does it mean to patiently endure in faith?

GOING DEEPER

We cannot see the end of things from the middle and must walk by faith, not by sight. The Lord will bring a greater good, his perfect plan, out of all the frustration we feel and out of all the evil we experience. When all is said and done, God uses even injustice to fulfill his promises to us. As Joseph explained to his brothers, "You intended to harm me, but God intended it for good" (Gen. 50:20). Paradoxically, Satan channeled wrath against Jesus through human agents who nailed him to the cross, but it was simultaneously God's work of atonement.[11]

RESPONDING TO GOD'S WORD

The Heidelberg Catechism[12] is a series of questions and answers, originally published in 1563, and used as a method of instruction to Christians about Reformed doctrine. Questions #27 and #28 of the catechism deal with the understanding of providence, which can be of great comfort when facing trials of many kinds. At such times, the support and encouragement of a small group of people who know you is incredibly important. Sometimes they can see things through God's eyes, or at least remind you of his faithfulness, when you can't do it yourself.

IN YOUR GROUP:

Read the catechism questions (below) together, then use this time to pray for one another, and don't neglect to remember each other in prayer during the week.

ON YOUR OWN:

After reading through the catechism questions (below), take time to name people in your life whom God has used to support and encourage you during difficult times. Spend a couple of minutes in prayer to thank God for them. If you have the opportunity, tell them so during the week!

27. Q. What do you understand by the providence of God?
    A. Providence is
        the almighty and ever present power of God[13]
        by which he upholds, as with his hand,
        heaven
        and earth
        and all creatures,[14]
        and so rules them that
        leaf and blade,
        rain and drought,
        fruitful and lean years,
        food and drink,
        health and sickness,
        prosperity and poverty—[15]

all things, in fact, come to us
not by chance[16]
but from his fatherly hand.[17]

28. Q. How does the knowledge of God's creation and providence help us?

A. We can be patient when things go against us,[18]
thankful when things go well,[19]
and for the future we can have
good confidence in our faithful God and Father
that nothing will separate us from his love.[20]
All creatures are so completely in his hand
that without his will
they can neither move nor be moved.[21]

NOTES

1. This section is based on *NIVAC: Esther*, 116–122.
2. Jobes, 119.
3. Jobes, 118.
4. Jobes, 118, 124.
5. Jobes, 120.
6. Ibid.
7. Jobes, 121.
8. This section is based on *NIVAC: Esther*, 122–129.
9. Jobes, 122.
10. Jobes, 125.
11. Jobes, 128.
12. Online May 9, 2007 at http://www.crcna.org/pages/heidelberg_father.cfm.
13. Jer. 23:23–24; Acts 17:24–28.
14. Heb. 1:3.
15. Jer. 5:24; Acts 14:15–17; John 9:3; Prov. 22:2.
16. Prov. 16:33.
17. Matt. 10:29.
18. Job 1:21–22; James 1:3.
19. Deut. 8:10; 1 Thess. 5:18.
20. Ps. 55:22; Rom. 5:3–5; 8:38–39.
21. Job 1:12; 2:6; Prov. 21:1; Acts 17:24–28.

BLOWING THE TRUMPET IN ZION

Esther 4:1–5:8

Have you ever experienced an identity crisis? In Western culture, that can be psychobabble for being unsure of ourselves. But there have been many people throughout history who have been persecuted because of their identity—whether because of faith, ethnicity, lifestyle, economic status, or other things. When revealing your identity becomes a matter of compromising who you are, sometimes to the point of life or death, who do you say you are? Haman's edict makes this an issue for the Jews, and Esther is no exception. After five years of hiding her Jewish identity, will she choose to identify with her people or try to hide in the Persian courts behind her title of queen? Although our circumstances might not be quite as drastic, God often challenges us as well—will we stand up as Christians, or try to blend in with the rest of the world?

ESTHER'S DILEMMA[1]

Read Esther 4:1–17.

1. The last scene ended in bewilderment over King Xerxes' edict "to destroy, kill and annihilate all the Jews—young and old, women and children—on ... the thirteenth day of the twelfth month" (Est. 3:13). How do Mordecai and the Jews of the Persian empire respond (4:1–3)? What is Esther's initial response (4:4)?

2. Mordecai wants Esther to beg the king for mercy for the Jews—who better than the queen to be in a position of influence? What difficulties does Esther foresee in Mordecai's plan (4:10–11)? Why?

3. Esther faces a dilemma. She risks probable death at the king's orders if she follows Mordecai's command, or certain death if she remains silent. In what way does this cause an identity crisis for Esther? Whom does Esther choose to identify with (4:15–16)?

4. How does Esther's response to Mordecai (4:15 – 16) differ from her previous interactions with him (see 2:10 and 2:20)? What prompts this change?

Up to this point in the story, while Esther was pretending to be a pagan, she was controlled by her circumstances. She has been passive in the story, not initiating action, but following along the path of least resistance. Then comes that defining moment when she is faced with taking responsibility for the life God has given her by identifying herself with the people of God. According to [Leland] Ryken, it is through this traumatic ordeal that Esther, "initially a beautiful young woman with a weak character, becomes transformed into a person with heroic moral stature and political skill."[2]

GOD'S WHISPERS[3]

Read Joel 1:13 – 15 and 2:12 – 14.

The Hebrew phrase translated in the [T]NIV of Esther 4:3 as "with fasting, weeping and wailing" occurs in both 4:3 and in Joel 2:12. (Of course, the individual words of this phrase occur many other times in the Old Testament.) This phrase forms an intertextual link between Esther and Joel. The author of Esther, in other words, tells this episode of the story using an allusive echo of Joel 2.[4]

5. There is no mention of God in the book of Esther, but the possible allu-
    sion to the prophet Joel suggests that Mordecai believed that God was
    fully engaged in the potential destruction that faced the Jews. How do
    Mordecai's actions reflect his identity as a Jew, particularly in light of the
    cited passages in Joel?

6. Compare Mordecai's language in Esther 4:14b with the prophet's language
    in Joel 2:14a. How might Mordecai's words have helped Esther in her
    defining moment?

Read Joel 2:15 – 16a.

7. In what sense did Esther "blow the trumpet in Zion"? What enabled her
    to do this?

GOING DEEPER

It is unlikely that any of us will ever be in Esther's dire predicament, but every one of us faces defining moments in our own lives. Certainly the most fundamental of them comes when we hear the gospel of Jesus Christ and decide to respond to it. The gospel confronts us with the decision either to continue to live as pagans or to identify ourselves with God's people, the church. Our choice defines who we are and with what people we identify. The decision to be identified with Christ energizes our lives. It gives us a purpose bigger than our own concerns and problems and a hope that goes beyond our own death.[5]

FOR SUCH A TIME AS THIS[6]

Read Esther 5:1–8.

8. How is the description of Esther in 5:1–2 different from her description in 2:15–16 and 4:10–11?

GOING DEEPER

The transformation of Esther's character from a person of "weak character" to one with "heroic moral stature and political skill" proceeds from that defining moment when she decides to identify herself with God's covenant.... Esther assumes the dignity and power of her royal position only after she claims her true identity as a woman of God.[7]

9. Rather than answering King Xerxes directly, Esther invites him, together with Haman, to a banquet. How is Esther's attitude toward the king (5:3–4) similar to that of his advisers? How is it different?

10. What character qualities does Esther exhibit as she assumes her dual role as God's instrument and queen of Persia?

Character transformation is a work of the Holy Spirit, who brings to fruition the qualities of love, joy, peace, patience, kindness, goodness, faithfulness, gentleness, and self-control in those who belong to Jesus Christ (Gal. 5:22–23). Without this transformation of character by the Holy Spirit, none of us can attain the full potential of our humanity. Without the work of God's Spirit, we cannot be the persons God created us to be, nor can we attain fully to the purpose of our lives as agents of God's redemptive work in history.[8]

11. What kind of character transformation do you see the Spirit performing in your own life? What events in your life promote such transformation?

12. Consider Mordecai's influence and interactions with Esther. How can you be a positive influence on others at defining moments in their lives?

RESPONDING TO GOD'S WORD

Haman was not the first or last enemy of God's people, nor was Esther the only child of God facing a defining moment "for such a time as this." In the fullness of time, there was one, Jesus Christ, whose identity was also hidden for a time, who faced a defining moment in the garden of Gethsemane. Given the choice of drinking the cup that would surely lead to his death, Jesus aligns himself with his Father's will in order to utterly defeat the enemy of God's people for all time.

IN YOUR GROUP:

Take a moment to reflect on the implications of this defining moment. Have each person write down on a slip of paper a sentence about something he or she is thankful for because of this defining moment in Christ's life. Have one person read the sentences aloud as a closing prayer, ending with Joel 2:13 (below).

ON YOUR OWN:

Take a moment to reflect on the implications of this defining moment, and give thanks to God who, through the death of his Son Jesus, gives us the opportunity to:

> *Rend your heart*
> *and not your garments.*
> *Return to the LORD your God,*
> *for he is gracious and compassionate,*
> *slow to anger and abounding in love,*
> *and he relents from sending calamity.*
>
> Joel 2:13

NOTES

1. This section is based on *NIVAC: Esther*, 130–134, 137–139.
2. Jobes, 138.
3. This section is based on *NIVAC: Esther*, 135–137.
4. Jobes, 135.
5. Jobes, 140–141.
6. This section is based on *NIVAC: Esther*, 139–150.
7. Jobes, 146.
8. Jobes, 148.

THE TABLES TURN

Esther 5:9 – 6:14

H ave you ever had the breath knocked out of you? A lot of times it happens in the middle of a fun activity, so it's all the more unexpected. You're having a great time, when all of a sudden, you fall down and think you're going to die—you can't catch your breath. Haman has a day like that—only worse! They say it's not what you know, but who you know that matters. Haman may have thought being "in" with the king was a good enough connection, but being an enemy of God's people was the real clincher for him. Ultimately, our lives rest in the hands of our unseen but sovereign God, who is ruling all of history. Who you know does indeed make all the difference, if you're on his side.

A HAPPY DAY FOR HAMAN[1]

Read Esther 5:9–14.

1. Haman is very pleased with himself following Esther's first banquet. You can almost see him holding himself a little taller, his chest puffing out just a bit more than it was before. What feeds Haman's pride (3:1 – 2; 5:11 – 12)? What one thing eats away at Haman's happiness (3:2; 5:9)?

2. Haman is delighted with the suggestion made by his wife Zeresh to erect a huge gallows (5:14). If only he had thought of it himself! Somehow he comes up with the resources to have this seventy-five-foot structure erected overnight. How are Haman's goals and plans consistent with what we have seen of his nature so far? How is his nature reflected in his conversation with the king the next morning (6:6)?

Haman's proposal for what "should be done for the man the king delights to honor" [6:6, [T]NIV] may seem unusual by modern standards. Believing the honors would go to himself, Haman could not ask for a promotion because he was already second only to the king in his authority over the empire. He apparently had all the wealth and luxury such a high-ranking position could afford in opulent Persia. His request to wear the king's robe and ride the king's horse was intended both to honor the king and to reinforce Haman's relationship with him.[2]

THE TABLES TURN[3]

Read Esther 6:1 – 14.

3. Who knows if King Xerxes was reading the book of the chronicles, the record of his reign, to induce sleep or ease his mind, but it has a big impact on the rest of the story. How does the king's sleepless night (6:1 – 3) affect the outcome of events?

The king's sleepless night is the pivot point of the literary structure of the story around which the great reversal of destiny occurs. . . . Since the book both begins and ends with pairs of feasts, it is striking that Esther also gives not one, but two banquets for the king and Haman. Haman's downfall begins between the first and second of Esther's banquets, when the king has a sleepless night. Thus there are three pairs of feasts that mark the beginning, the climax, and the conclusion of the story.[4]

4. In Esther 3, the role of "chance" (e.g., the roll of the *purim*) was discussed relative to other Scriptures, such as Proverbs 16:33: "The lot is cast into the lap, but its every decision is from the LORD." How does this concept affect the understanding of the king's sleepless night? Who is really governing the action at the pivot point of the book of Esther?

GOING DEEPER

In spite of having all the power of the Persian empire at his disposal, Haman's carefully laid plans were turned against him simply because the king had a sleepless night! The author is suggesting that beneath the surface of human decisions and actions is an unseen and uncontrollable power at work, which can be neither explained nor thwarted.... Read from a monotheistic perspective, the story explains the reversal of fortune not as an ongoing tug-of-war between the gods, but as consistent with the powerful word of the one, true God. The author of Esther implies a consistency in God's rule of human history that is based on his word, not on circumstances. Regardless of how circumstances appear, God is ruling history according to the ancient covenant he made with Israel at Sinai.[5]

5. "This is arguably the most ironically comic scene in the entire Bible."[6] At last, Mordecai is recognized for exposing the assassination plot against King Xerxes. What is Mordecai's long overdue reward, and how is it determined (6:6–10)?

6. From ecstasy to agony! Could the contrast of two days in a person's life be any greater? Describe the reversals that occur in Haman's life before and after the king's sleepless night.

GOING DEEPER

[Peripety is] a literary term that refers to a sudden turn of events in a story that reverses the intended and expected action.... The narrative tension of the conflict between the Jews of Persia and their enemy, Haman, is not simply resolved, it is resolved through reversals. Haman's plan could have simply been stopped and the status quo preserved. Instead, there is a great reversal of fortune. An event intended to harm the Jews actually results in the opposite, against every expectation. Instead of being destroyed, the Jewish people are not only delivered, but empowered through the high rank of Esther and Mordecai. The empowered destroyer, Haman, not only loses his power, but is himself destroyed.[7]

7. Haman's wife, Zeresh, almost sounds like a prophetess. She sees and understands the very essence of Haman's problem: "Since Mordecai, before whom your downfall has started, is of Jewish origin, you cannot stand against him — you will surely come to ruin!" (6:13). How does this reversal of fortune speak to the activity of God in the lives of his dispersed people?

GOING DEEPER

The reversal of destiny that began when the king had a sleepless night implies that, despite their sin and despite their location away from Jerusalem, God's promise to Israel made at the beginning of their nation still stood. God was not capricious like the gods of the pagans. He was not locked in some struggle with other deities that gave him control only on certain days or in certain situations. All that had happened was consistent with the stated provisions of God's covenant.[8]

8. God has not been mentioned in the entire book of Esther, but we have given him a lot of credit for his behind-the-scenes activities. What have you learned about God's character from the book of Esther up to this point?

9. The Jews in Persia were part of the scattered people of Israel, located there because of their disobedience for many generations in the chosen land that God had given them. But they were not the first people to disobey God. How does the predicament of the exiled Jews mirror the predicament of all of humankind as a result of the activities and choices in the garden of Eden?

GOING DEEPER

We should expect nothing but death, but we have seen the ultimate peripety, the ultimate reversal of expected ends, in another seemingly ordinary human event: the birth of a baby in Bethlehem and the execution of that man on a cross. The ordinary and the miraculous intersect in Jesus Christ. Because of the death and resurrection of Jesus Christ, our destiny has been reversed from death to life against all expectation. The cross of Jesus Christ is the pivot point of the great reversal of history, where our sorrow has been turned to joy.[9]

10. God doesn't change. The faithful activity of God in the lives of his people in Persia (despite their disobedience) is not a one-time event. Israel's history and the church's history are one. In light of such great news, what can God's chosen people today expect regarding God's activity in their lives (see Rom. 8:35 – 39)?

11. Consider how God has guided and directed your life. What unexpected events, good or bad, have led you in directions you didn't anticipate?

GOING DEEPER

It is particularly appropriate for the pivot point of the peripety that reverses the expected outcome to occur at an ordinary and insignificant event in a book whose meta-message is about divine providence. God providentially directs the flow of human history through the ordinary lives of individuals to fulfill the promises of his covenant. What a great God we serve! Any deity worth his salt can do a miracle now and then. Our God is so great, so powerful, that he can work without miracles through the ordinary events of billions of human lives through millennia of time to accomplish his eternal purposes and ancient promises.[10]

RESPONDING TO GOD'S WORD

John Newton is one example of many whose providential, seemingly insignificant life-events were used by God to bring about a radical personal transformation. From promising start to abused orphan, John Newton became a hardened seaman and eventually master of his own slave ship. When he hit a violent storm that nearly sunk his ship, John Newton experienced his "great deliverance." The worst of circumstances turned his life around and steered him toward greater things. He wrote over 250 hymns, some of which continue on in our tradition to this day, helping us to reflect on the God who uses ordinary circumstances to bring about amazing change in our lives. Newton's most famous hymn, "Amazing Grace,"[11] is familiar even to many outside the Christian faith.

IN YOUR GROUP:

Read through the words to "Amazing Grace" first, so you can think about them. Then sing this hymn together and give praise to God for the amazing grace he has shown in your own life.

ON YOUR OWN:

Think about the words in this hymn and sing out your praise to God for the amazing grace he has shown in your life.

AMAZING GRACE

Amazing grace! How sweet the sound
That saved a wretch like me!
I once was lost, but now am found,
Was blind, but now I see.

'Twas grace that taught my heart to fear,
And grace my fears relieved;
How precious did that grace appear
the hour I first believed!

Through many dangers, toils and snares
I have already come;
'Twas grace that brought me safe thus far
and grace will lead me home.

The Lord has promised good to me
His Word my hope secures;
He will my Shield and Portion be,
as long as life endures.

When we've been there ten thousand years
bright shining as the sun,
We've no less days to sing God's praise
than when we'd first begun.

NOTES

1. This section is based on *NIVAC: Esther*, 145–146.
2. Jobes, 153.
3. This section is based on *NIVAC: Esther*, 151–162.
4. Jobes, 154–155.
5. Jobes, 158–159.
6. Jobes, 152.
7. Jobes, 155–156.
8. Jobes, 159.
9. Jobes, 161.
10. Jobes, 159–160.
11. Online July 19, 2007 at http://www.cyberhymnal.org/htm/a/m/a/amazing_grace.htm.

PRIDE GOES BEFORE A FALL

Esther 7:1–10

In Gilbert and Sullivan's *The Mikado*, the Japanese emperor contemplates what it means to find "the punishment that fits the crime." In chapter 7, King Xerxes faces the same dilemma, and Haman unwittingly helps him come up with a quick solution for his own demise. Unfortunately, a lot of personal and political motives get intertwined in corrupt governments and true justice is often skirted. But all of us need to think carefully about perfect justice — it can get us in trouble when we apply it as honestly to ourselves as we do to other people. It's really easy to fool ourselves into thinking how right we are in all kinds of situations, when we're really just promoting our own agendas, not God's. God's perfect justice would mean the end of all of us if it weren't for his own intervention for those he loves!

HAMAN'S LAST BANQUET[1]

Read Esther 7:1–10.

1. At Esther's second banquet, King Xerxes repeats his generous offer to
    Queen Esther for the third time (see also 5:3, 6), "What is your petition?
    It will be given you. What is your request? Even up to half the kingdom,
    it will be granted" (7:2). It would seem as if Esther has King Xerxes in the
    palm of her hand. How does Esther's response in 7:3 parallel the language
    of King Xerxes? How is Esther's identity reflected in her response?

2. Queen Esther's explanation (7:4) is in the passive voice, demonstrating
    good judgment considering the circumstances. Why is it a good idea for
    her to choose her words carefully?

3. The king certainly seems willing to grant Esther anything, but Esther's
    request is rather unusual and no doubt unexpected. Why might Queen
    Esther's request cause a dilemma for King Xerxes?

4. The beginning of the reversal of Haman's expected fortune hit hard in the last chapter, but the specifics come through in brilliant color in this chapter. What he thought started out as a bad day just gets worse and worse. What specific elements in the story are reversed (see 3:1, 5; 5:14; 6:4)?

GOING DEEPER The scene is steeped in irony. Consider how the entire conflict between Haman and the Jewish people begins when Mordecai the Jew dishonors Haman the Agagite by refusing to fall before him. In his final scene, Haman falls before a Jew (and a Jewish woman at that!), whom he has unknowingly condemned to death, to plead with her for his life! On the couch of this Jewish queen he "falls" all the way from his exalted position as second over the empire to an ignominious death as a traitor.[2]

5. For all his faults, Haman really had no way to know what he was getting himself into. And yet, he is still responsible for his actions. How has Haman brought his judgment upon himself? In what ways was it beyond his control?

6. The sentence for Haman is death by hanging, but what exactly is he guilty of? It might depend on whom you talk to. What is Haman actually guilty of in King Xerxes' eyes? In Queen Esther's or Mordecai's eyes? In God's eyes?

GOING DEEPER

Harem protocol dictated that no one but the king could be left alone with a woman of the harem. Haman should have left Esther's presence when the king retreated to the garden, but where could he have gone? His choice was either to follow the king, who had bolted in anger from his presence, or to flee the room, suggesting guilt and inviting pursuit. Haman is trapped. Even in the presence of others, a man was not to approach a woman of the king's harem within seven steps. That Haman should actually fall on the couch where Esther is reclining is unthinkable!... Precisely at this moment of impropriety Xerxes returns and finds his quandary about what to do with Haman resolved.... Regardless of intent, Haman has undeniably violated harem protocol, a serious affront to the king himself and reason enough to condemn him to death.[3]

7. Haman was hanged from a gallows of his own making, seventy-five feet high, the same day he honored Mordecai in the streets of Susa, and the same day he attended Esther's exclusive banquet with the king. Do you think he deserved his fate? Why or why not? Is it consistent with Haman's own sense of justice?

8. The ultimate victory of Esther and the defeat of Haman are connected with their identity with a group of people—God's chosen or God's enemy. Does this justify Esther's revenge against Haman? Would her actions be pleasing to God?

9. Do Esther's actions justify revenge on those who have intended harm in your own life? Explain.

GOING DEEPER

While reflecting on who gets life and who does not, the author of Esther reveals that life and death are determined by identification with a people.... In New Testament theology, life and death are also shown to be by identification with a people. The work of Jesus Christ is the consummation of God's covenant promises to ancient Israel (2 Cor. 1:20). Thus, the ultimate fulfillment of God's promise to his people for protection from death is found in Jesus Christ. Identification with him constitutes a people who will be delivered from death and live forever, just as Jesus was.[4]

10. The face we show to others is not always the same as the way we see ourselves. To what extent do you identify with the people of God? Would others identify you as a person of God? What implications does your identity as a Christian have on your day-to-day actions and attitudes?

11. We tend to be quick to assess the good or evil in others, but much slower to see it accurately in ourselves. Can you think of a time in your life when you were convinced in what you were doing, only to realize later that it was not of God?

GOING DEEPER

Haman's example shows that human evil is self-deceptive. It allows evildoers to believe themselves justified in their evil actions and clever enough not to get caught in their own web. Haman had all the resources of the empire on his side as he schemed and plotted—power, prestige, wealth—but it all came to nothing because of that one unforeseen, unpredictable night of the king's insomnia.... Evil is also self-deceptive because while it appears to provide well-being and safety, it feeds off impulses that blind us to the truth. Haman's true, precarious situation was veiled to him by the darkness of his own thinking.... For Haman, things were actually not what they appeared to be, even while he himself was doing them. Suddenly, without warning, the true destiny of human evil is revealed: destruction by the long-promised justice of God. On the final judgment day when the truth is revealed, the condemned will finally realize that they have no one to blame but themselves.[5]

RESPONDING TO GOD'S WORD

King David did a great job of deceiving himself about the evil he did in regard to Bathsheba and her first husband, until Nathan the prophet made him come to his senses (2 Sam. 11–12). David wrote Psalm 51 in response to the realization of his sin, identifying with God and his people in spite of the actions that essentially set him against God.

IN YOUR GROUP:

Read through the psalm responsively, making it your own prayer as you think about ways in which you also have set yourself against the Lord and his plans.

ON YOUR OWN:

As you read through the psalm, make it your own prayer as you think about ways in which you also have set yourself against the Lord and his plans. Praise him for the mercy he has shown us through Jesus' death, cleansing us to be "whiter than snow."

PSALM 51

For the director of music. A psalm of David. When the prophet Nathan came to him after David had committed adultery with Bathsheba.

¹Have mercy on me, O God,
according to your unfailing love;
according to your great compassion
blot out my transgressions.
²Wash away all my iniquity
and cleanse me from my sin.
³For I know my transgressions,
and my sin is always before me.
⁴Against you, you only, have I sinned
and done what is evil in your sight;
so you are right in your verdict
and justified when you judge.

⁵*Surely I was sinful at birth,*
   sinful from the time my mother conceived me.
⁶*Yet you desired faithfulness even in the womb;*
   you taught me wisdom in that secret place.
⁷*Cleanse me with hyssop, and I will be clean;*
   wash me, and I will be whiter than snow.
⁸*Let me hear joy and gladness;*
   let the bones you have crushed rejoice.
⁹*Hide your face from my sins*
   and blot out all my iniquity.
¹⁰*Create in me a pure heart, O God,*
   and renew a steadfast spirit within me.
¹¹*Do not cast me from your presence*
   or take your Holy Spirit from me.
¹²*Restore to me the joy of your salvation*
   and grant me a willing spirit, to sustain me.
¹³*Then I will teach transgressors your ways,*
   and sinners will turn back to you.
¹⁴*Deliver me from bloodguilt, O God,*
   you who are God my Savior,
   and my tongue will sing of your righteousness.
¹⁵*Open my lips, Lord,*
   and my mouth will declare your praise.
¹⁶*You do not delight in sacrifice, or I would bring it;*
   you do not take pleasure in burnt offerings.
¹⁷*My sacrifice, O God, is a broken spirit;*
   a broken and contrite heart
   you, God, will not despise.
¹⁸*May it please you to prosper Zion,*
   to build up the walls of Jerusalem.
¹⁹*Then you will delight in the sacrifices of the righteous,*
   in burnt offerings offered whole;
   then bulls will be offered on your altar.

NOTES

1. This section is based on *NIVAC: Esther*, 163–174.
2. Jobes, 166–167.
3. Jobes, 165–166.
4. Jobes, 173–174.
5. Jobes, 173.

A REVERSAL OF FORTUNE

Esther 8:1–17

What does a holy God think of holy war, and how are we, as his followers, supposed to think about it? It's easy to point out mistakes that have been made in history in the name of God, but we often get confused about what's actually in the Bible. Was it right? Was it wrong? Have things changed? Can we use biblical history to defend the actions of nations today? What does it mean to love my enemy? Wrestling with these questions is hard and can easily polarize people. But given the end of the book of Esther, we can't avoid the subject.

HOPE FOR THE JEWS[1]

Read Esther 8:1–17.

1. Esther's petition and request to the king (7:3–4) was for her life and the lives of her people, the Jews. What was King Xerxes' response to the request (7:10–8:1)? Did the king honor Esther's request? Explain.

2. What aspect of Persian law made it difficult for King Xerxes to grant Esther's request (8:8)? How did he get around the law?

GOING DEEPER

There has been much discussion in the commentaries whether it is historically true that the laws of Persian kings were irrevocable, since there is no extrabiblical attestation in Herodotus or other sources of this practice.... Even if the author is using poetic license by introducing this element of irrevocability, perhaps he is making a theological point about human destiny. Just as Xerxes king of Persia could not simply rescind the first decree of death, God, King of the universe, cannot simply rescind the decree of death pronounced in the garden of Eden against humanity. Instead, he issues a counter-decree of life, the gospel of Jesus Christ.[2]

3. Compare Mordecai's decree (8:11) with Haman's decree (3:13). In what ways do the Jews behave similarly to their enemies? How are they different?

4. When Mordecai's counter-decree was issued to the entire Persian empire, "it was a time of happiness and joy, gladness and honor" for the Jews (8:16), even though no one had raised a hand against them yet. Were the Jews "counting their chickens before they hatched?" Why might they feel this way?

5. The response of the Jews to Mordecai's edict was, naturally enough, a complete turnaround from their response to Haman's original edict to annihilate the Jews. What other reversals have come to fruition in this chapter?

Before	After
Est. 3:10	Est. 8:2
Est. 3:12	Est. 8:9–10
Est. 3:13	Est. 8:11
Est. 3:14	Est. 8:13
Est. 3:15	Est. 8:14, 15b
Est. 4:1	Est. 8:15a

6. In the Sermon on the Mount, Jesus countered the idea of hating your enemy with, "But I tell you, love your enemies and pray for those who persecute you" (Matt. 5:44). In Luke 6:35, Jesus took it one step further, "Love your enemies, do good to them, and lend to them without expecting to get anything back. Then your reward will be great, and you will be children of the Most High, because he is kind to the ungrateful and wicked." Given this New Testament teaching, how would you regard Mordecai's decree today? Has God's message changed?

HOLY WAR![3]

The concept of holy war is not unique to Esther. Read Deuteronomy 9:1–6, which takes place prior to the original occupation of Canaan by the Israelites.

7. God could hardly be clearer in these verses as to why he wants to destroy the nations occupying the Promised Land. What was the basis for the holy war declared on the Anakites (Deut. 9:4–5)?

8. What qualified the Jews to be the agents of God's destruction on the Anakites (as well as other tribes that occupied the Promised Land at that time)?

GOING DEEPER

Whether we like it or not, the Old Testament is full of God's violence against the nations, who are portrayed as being such evil and sinful people that their destruction is the only remedy.... The destruction of Sodom and Gomorrah and other nations in the Old Testament shows that in truth as only God can see it, there are no "good" people who by their own merit are undeserving of destruction. The Old Testament stories of death and destruction illustrate the New Testament teaching, "For all have sinned and fall short of the glory of God," and "the wages of sin is death" (Rom. 3:23; 6:23).[4]

GOD'S COUNTER-DECREE AGAINST SIN[5]

Read Isaiah 59:12–17.

9. Life in the garden of Eden started out fine, but then Adam and Eve were kicked out. God started a new nation through Abraham, but that didn't go perfectly either. In fact, you could say things just go from bad to worse in the Old Testament. But the prophets, including Isaiah, hint at something different in the future. You could say a reversal occurs, just as we have seen in the book of Esther. What aspects of redemptive history have been reversed, mirroring the book of Esther? How was this accomplished?

God's irrevocable decree of death and destruction has been countered by his decree that all who believe in his Son should not perish under his wrath but be delivered into eternal life. The violence of God against sin and evil can therefore be rightly understood only "in the shadow of the cross." Jesus Christ is the ultimate divine warrior and king of Israel, who waged the final war against sin and evil on the cross on behalf of the people God will deliver from final destruction.[6]

10. Look at question 6 again. Think about God's "weapon of choice" against his enemies in the Old Testament and the New Testament. Considering God's means of action as a divine warrior, how can you reconcile the Old Testament understanding of holy war with the New Testament regard for enemies?

The death of Jesus Christ, the Messiah of Israel, provides the only basis for the cessation of holy war, and the infilling of the Holy Spirit provides the only power by which one may love one's enemies as oneself. All of the vengeance God's people would like to wreak on those who practice evil has now been satisfied in the suffering and death of Jesus. He has taken the wages of sin, he has suffered the vengeance of evil. The vengeance due to us for our sins against others and due to them for their sins against us has been satisfied in Jesus' body on the cross. It is only on the basis of recognizing that the penalty has been paid by Jesus that we can forgive others as we have been forgiven. True holy war in human history has ceased because Jesus has fought its last episode on the cross.[7]

11. As a Christian today, how might you participate as a holy warrior who would bring "happiness and joy, gladness and honor" (Est. 8:16) to yourself, to others, and to the God whom you serve (see Eph. 6:10–18)? What are we called to actually fight now?

GOING DEEPER

The church of Jesus Christ replaces the army of Israel as the agency of God that wars against sin and evil in the world, and the theater of the battle has moved to the human heart, where sin and evil reside.[8]

RESPONDING TO GOD'S WORD

God has not only brought about a reversal in redemptive history, but also in individual lives.

IN YOUR GROUP:

Is there a pivotal point in your story in which God "turned the tables" on you? Are there reversals you can specifically point to in your own life after God caused a change in your heart? Take time in your group to share your answers with one another. This might be a good time to plan an extra gathering with time specifically set aside to share testimonies and celebrate the ways God has brought about change in your lives.

ON YOUR OWN:

Make a timeline for yourself. Is there a pivotal point in your story in which God "turned the tables" on you? Are there reversals you can specifically point to in your own life after God caused a change in your heart? Take time to celebrate the things God has done in your life and pray about the things that you recognize still need "reversing." Share your thoughts with someone else as a way of testifying to God's work in your life.

NOTES

1. This section is based on *NIVAC: Esther*, 175 – 183.
2. Jobes, 188 – 189.
3. This section is based on *NIVAC: Esther*, 183 – 188.
4. Jobes, 187 – 188.
5. This section is based on *NIVAC: Esther*, 188 – 193.
6. Jobes, 191.
7. Jobes, 184.
8. Jobes, 192.

LET THE
CELEBRATION
BEGIN!

Esther 9:1–10:3

N ext time Purim rolls around, usually in March, you'll have more reason to celebrate! It's an event that Jews still look forward to, and celebrate with great gusto and fun in their synagogues. As Christians, we have been adopted into the history of the Old Testament, and have our own reasons to celebrate — not just for the preservation of a remnant of God's people in Persia, but for the message it has for us in the way it points to Christ.

VICTORY FOR THE JEWS[1]

Read Esther 9:1 – 19.

1. The Jews started celebrating way before their battle even started, hinting at the victory to come (8:16–17). How else does the story of Esther foreshadow victory for the Jews? Was the outcome guaranteed? Explain.

2. The big day arrives and everyone seems to be shaking in their boots for fear of the Jews. How do the Jews treat their enemies (9:5–10)? Is this consistent with the king's edict (8:11)? Why or why not?

GOING DEEPER

The author is careful to say three times that the Jews "did not lay their hands on the plunder" (vv. 10, 15, 16) even though Mordecai's decree allowed it. Mordecai's decree included the permission to plunder because he was reversing the exact terms that Haman's decree had previously established. However, unlike the Agagite's intent, the Jews understood the execution of Mordecai's decree as governed by the ancient command of holy war against the Amalekites. One of the rules of ancient holy war was that plunder must not be taken.... Echoes of Saul's failure resound throughout this episode of how the Jews got the upper hand and finally destroyed Haman the Agagite, who was effectively, if not formally, the "king" of their enemies. Thus, under the leadership of Esther and Mordecai, the Jews of Persia obeyed where King Saul had disobeyed and did to their enemies as the Lord had commanded so long before.[2]

3. The Jews are victorious and King Xerxes reports on the battle casualties to Esther. Everything seems to be wrapping up nicely, but then the king repeats his offer to Esther for anything she wants. How does Esther respond to the king's further offer (9:13)? What does this say to you about her character?

GOING DEEPER

The biblical Esther is evaluated almost universally in negative terms for requesting a second day of killing.... If tradition is correct, it is perhaps after this incident that the people nicknamed their queen "Esther" alluding to Ishtar, the Babylonian goddess of love and war.

The Bible is remarkable in revealing the darker side of God's chosen leaders, often just at their shining moment.... If the second day of killing happened because of a darker side to Esther's character, the author does not attempt to vindicate her. Perhaps he is suggesting that no one, Jew or Gentile, can handle power without yielding to its dark side. Perhaps Esther's request for a second day of killing shows that she herself had begun to feel the heady intoxication of the power she had so remarkably attained. Even as others in the courts have manipulated Xerxes for their own agendas, Esther also has now learned to exercise her power over Xerxes for her own purposes.

On the other hand, Esther's reasons for the second day of killing in Susa may have been legitimate, even though they are unknown to us, and were also possibly unknown to the author.... Esther's request is another instance of the disquieting moral ambiguity that characterizes this story. Rather than attempting to resolve it, we should reflect on it.[3]

4. In other episodes of holy war in the Bible, God is much more explicitly named and involved than in the book of Esther. To what extent would you say that God's hand is evident in the outcome of the events in Esther? To what extent are the Jews responsible for the outcome?

5. Compare the victory of the Jews in the book of Esther with the Jews' first victory against the Amalekites in Exodus 17:8–16. How is God's involvement similar? How is it different?

THE CELEBRATION OF PURIM[4]

Read Esther 9:20–28.

6. It is Mordecai who establishes Purim as a day of celebration for the Jews (9:20–22). How does his decree contribute to the significance of the victory as a work of God's hand? How is his written record of the event different from the one following the battle mentioned in Exodus 17:8–16?

7.   Purim is established much later than most other Jewish feasts, at a time when the people of Israel don't live anywhere near the Promised Land anymore. How does the celebration of Purim speak of God's relationship with his people at this point in history?

GOING DEEPER

Purim joined the five Jewish feasts that were commanded by Moses in the Torah and celebrated miraculous events surrounding the formation of the nation of Israel as God's covenant people. Purim commemorates the survival of that covenant nation, even though it was dispersed in the judgment of the exile centuries later.... The authority on which Purim is based is unlike that of the feasts commanded by Moses in the Pentateuch. Mordecai was not a prophet or a miracle worker, nor did he rule as king in Jerusalem. He wore the signet ring of a Persian king, not the ephod of the high priest. Mordecai simply wrote letters to the Jews throughout Persia describing the remarkable events that had transpired in the palace at Susa, leading to the deliverance, and the people then responded collectively to their shared experience.... The celebration of Purim is therefore different from the feasts prescribed by the Torah. Rather than being imposed on the people from above as God's commandment, Purim began as the spontaneous response of God's people to his omnipotent faithfulness to the promises of the covenant.[5]

8. Purim is a joyous celebration, even today, remembering that "on this day the enemies of the Jews had hoped to overpower them, but now the tables were turned and the Jews got the upper hand over those who hated them" (9:1). How does this foreshadow the resurrection?

9. God performed many signs and wonders in Israel's earlier history, and also in Jesus' ministry on earth. His involvement with his people was obvious at the time to believers as well as unbelievers. Esther's time in history as well as our own are different. We have to rely on the old stories, or much more subtle actions that we give God credit for. How is this a challenge to faith? How might it strengthen faith?

GOING DEEPER

Hebrews 11:1 defines faith as "being sure of what we hope for and *certain of what we do not see*" (emphasis added). In other words, the very definition of faith calls us to a certainty in the unseen reality lying behind, or beyond, the events we do see, even when, and perhaps especially when, the events are so incompatible with what we would expect given God's power and presence. Therefore, on what is our certainty to rest, if not on the visible events of history and life? It rests on the explanation God gives us of the unseen reality behind the visible events, that is, on God's Word. We move from indeterminacy to certainty only on the basis of God's Word.[6]

10. The author of Esther emphasizes how important it is to observe the celebration of Purim in every generation, every year (9:23–28). What might be an equivalent celebration for Christians? Why is it important to celebrate such events and pass them on to the next generation?

ORDINARY PEOPLE IN EXTRAORDINARY ROLES[7]

Read Esther 9:29–10:3.

11. Esther and Mordecai play a prominent role in God's plan for the Jews, although they are by no means perfect in action or motive, are not even particularly religious on the surface, and certainly do not qualify for any specific religious office such as priest or prophet. What does this say about the role of laity in the church today? What does it say about your role in God's plan?

12. Opinions are divided as to whether the main character of this book is Esther or Mordecai, but in actuality their roles depend on one another for the deliverance of God's people. How is their partnership similar to that of men and women in today's church? How is it different? What can we learn from their roles?

RESPONDING TO GOD'S WORD

Purim is a joyous holiday on the Jewish calendar that celebrates God's sovereign power to determine the destiny of those who are his. Many songs and poems have been written for its celebration, such as the one below.

IN YOUR GROUP:

Compare Mordecai's role with what Jesus has done. Think about how you would rewrite this Purim song in light of the cross, and share your thoughts with the group in celebration of the joyful hope realized in the resurrection of Jesus.

ON YOUR OWN:

Reflect on how you would rewrite this Purim song[8] in light of the cross:

The Rose of Jacob was radiant and joyful
when men saw Mordecai arrayed in purple.
Their saviour You have been,
their hope in every generation.

You have shown that all who hope in You
will not be disappointed,
and all who trust in You will never be put to shame.
Cursed be Haman, who sought to destroy me,
blessed be Mordecai the Jew.
Cursed be Zeresh, the wife of my foe,
blessed be Esther, who was a shield for me,
and may Harbonah, too, be remembered for good!

NOTES

1. This section is based on *NIVAC: Esther*, 194–211.
2. Jobes, 196, 199.
3. Jobes, 201–202.
4. This section is based on *NIVAC: Esther*, 212–221.
5. Jobes, 213–214.
6. Jobes, 209.
7. This section is based on *NIVAC: Esther*, 222–231.
8. Robert Gordis, *Megillat Esther* (New York: Ktav, 1974), 93–97. Quoted in Jobes, 219.

LEADER'S NOTES

SESSION 1 LEADER'S NOTES

Just as the first chapter of Esther sets the stage for God's unfolding drama in this story, this session sets the stage for your study of the book of Esther. It's important to think about the story as the original audience would have understood it. The historical background included here will help you with that perspective. This story is a part of God's unfolding story of redemption. Therefore it's important to think about how the events of Esther point ahead to Christ as the climax of God's story centuries later. This will help you to make appropriate application to our contemporary setting as well.

This session in particular has a lot to say about the use of power in different settings. But be careful not to read your own questions and biases into the text. Let the text speak for itself, and then look at similarities to your own world. Finally, be sure to take the time (and encourage those in your class or group) to respond to what God is teaching you. God did not give his Word as an academic exercise, but to change us. This takes time and intentional thought, something we often neglect in our busy lives. Pray that the Holy Spirit would guide you as you study and reflect on God's Word in this session.

1. Xerxes is extremely powerful, wealthy, self-centered, and showy, but generous as well. The military leaders and nobles may have been sufficiently impressed to throw their lot in with the king. The least of the kingdom probably just enjoyed a good time, which may have induced greater loyalty to him.

2. Nations rise and fall. No one but God is everlasting and all-powerful, but a national leader needs more than wealth and loyalty for continued success. Reading the story after Xerxes' defeat as the original readers would have read it also introduces one of the key themes that appear throughout the book: how a sudden turn of events can abruptly change an expected outcome (the literary term for such an unexpected reversal is "peripety").

3. At a time when King Xerxes is trying to impress the nobles, military leaders, and the people of the empire to rally support for his campaign against Greece, disobedience by his wife and queen would undermine his goals and be extremely embarrassing.

4. The author makes no ethical judgments on this interaction. Some scholars have used this section to argue against the evils of alcohol, or rebellious wives, but to do so is bringing our own questions and assumptions into the story, rather than taking the cues of the author to guide our understanding. In the context of this book, the author is saying less about marriage and more about the king's power.[1]

5. Esther will be entering a politically charged atmosphere where women are expected to be beautiful and obedient, not independent or opinionated. It points to the tremendous odds Esther will face.

6. Xerxes' advisers seem rather foolish in this instance. They seem motivated by self-interest rather than the concerns of the king, whether political or personal. Perhaps they had difficulty with their own wives! However, trying to legislate respect in a marriage is likely to result in just the opposite.

7. Although input from advisers is generally a good thing, the king's reliance on these particular advisers suggests a certain weakness and lack of discernment on the part of Xerxes.

8. Ironically, Xerxes guarantees that his wife's embarrassing action and his lack of control over her will be communicated to every household in his kingdom.

9. As stated in question 6, trying to legislate respect in a marriage is likely to result in just the opposite. God's foundation for respect in Ephesians 5 is mutual submission (v. 21) and love. Clearly, godly love will promote greater unity within a marriage than any royal decree.

10. The Persian empire was a mix of many nationalities and languages. It was probably wise for a minority group not to stand out too much. The

Jews, living in such a pluralistic society, would be influenced by the king as well as the many other nationalities of people around them. In Nehemiah's time, there is evidence that intermarriage occurred between Jews and many other peoples, so it must have been happening here as well. Although there were some who no doubt held on to the Jewish way of life, it would be easy to begin to blend in with everyone else, especially when there was no system in place for regulating Jewish law. We'll see this as an issue in Esther's life in the next chapter.

11. Xerxes' kingdom, like all human nations, is a shallow and broken image of God's kingdom. The Persian king's power and wealth hint at God's glorious kingdom, but Xerxes' leadership is marred by human sinfulness and greed. Jesus came and turned kingdom expectations upside down as a servant leader, and amazed people with the wisdom and authority he displayed, truly reflecting God's image. Psalm 2 says that God laughs, rebukes, and terrifies kings such as Xerxes, who come and go while God continues to unfold his everlasting purposes.

12. Although none of us wield the same kind of power as King Xerxes, we all make decisions that affect others. Some decisions affect those who are "below," or in submission to us. Other decisions are a response to those in authority over us or superior to us. The more specific you can be in considering applicable situations in your life, the more insight you'll have on the far-reaching impact of your day-to-day words and actions.

NOTE

1. For further discussion, see the "Bridging Contexts" section for 1:9–12, Jobes, 68.

SESSION 2 LEADER'S NOTES

The circumstances that surround our lives often make living out our faith a complex endeavor. What seems black and white in theory is much harder to apply in the details of real life. While looking at Esther's interesting yet complicated circumstances, think about your own choices in life and how they affect the living out of your faith.

1. So far, King Xerxes' laws have only promoted his own personal gain (and perhaps that of his advisers). His absolute authority has helped him, not his kingdom. In fact, it could be said that he has actually ruined the lives of hundreds of his subjects.[1]

2. It would seem extremely unlikely for a Jewish girl to have any sort of impact on the Persian nation. Understanding this helps to underline the turn of events that occurs in the book of Esther, as well as God's role in providentially ordering events on behalf of his people. No wonder this story was thought worthy to be preserved for all time!

3. Esther is characterized by her beauty. In addition, her obedience and submission to Mordecai and Hegai should be noted. The details are vague as to how she accomplishes it, but it's clear that "Esther won the favor of everyone who saw her" (2:15), including, and perhaps especially, the king.

4. Esther apparently blends in completely with the Persians, since her identity as a Jew went unnoticed. This implies that her dress, mannerisms, language, and any other cultural identifiers all blended in with Persian culture. The text is silent as to whether she honored the Jewish Sabbath, food laws, or any other distinctions. Certainly she did not keep herself pure regarding marriage to a Jew. Mordecai went along with the plan, which from a purely Jewish perspective would be frowned upon.[2]

5. God calls us to live in specific ways not to be legalistic or overbearing but for our own benefit, whether physically or spiritually. Many of the Jewish laws point to God's holiness and our dependence on him for all things. Our faith can suffer without daily reminders of God and how he wants us to live, honoring him and others. But God uses all our actions, faithful or otherwise, for his purposes. The author of Esther is silent as to condemning or condoning her actions.

6. Does the end justify the means? Esther and Mordecai faced a complex situation in which "the right answer" might not have been very clear to them.[3]

7. God's character and how he works on behalf of his people is intrinsic to the story of Esther. Not mentioning him by name is a clever literary tool emphasizing the historical circumstances of the exile.

8. This will vary from culture to culture in today's world. In Western culture, Christians are often indistinguishable from the culture, yet the Christian is clearly instructed to be distinct from the world (e.g., Eph. 4:17; Rom. 12:2). Many Christians would do well to think more seriously about the implications of this today.

9. Different Christians will likely answer this question in different ways, depending on their interpretation of Scripture, but it is nonetheless an important issue. It's also critical to think through carefully when cultures intersect, such as in missionary contexts. Sometimes living in a culture different from our own causes us to realize just how much we blur the lines between culture or tradition and faith.

10. As you think about difficult situations in your own life and the grace God has shown you, it can help you to be more compassionate toward others in different, but similarly complex situations.

NOTES

1. For further discussion, see Jobes, 94 – 95.
2. See Jobes, 101.
3. For further discussion, see Jobes, 106 – 108.

SESSION 3 LEADER'S NOTES

We all like to think we are in control of our lives, but every so often we are shaken to our very being with events that are completely outside our control. God's people need to remember that God's promises are reliable, and look back on history to understand how this can be true, even when things seem to be going against us.

1. Mordecai is a Jew of the tribe of Benjamin, son of Jair, son of Shimei, son of Kish, taken captive with Jehoiachin, king of Judah. He may be a distant relative of King Saul, son of Kish, the Benjamite.

2. Mordecai uncovers an assassination plot against the king. It is the first event we see respecting life and justice with no direct personal gain.

3. Mordecai should have been rewarded for his actions. It's an ironic twist for Haman to be rewarded for no given reason.

4. Haman is an Agagite (son of Hammedatha). Agag was king of the Amalekites, an enemy of King Saul.

5. "[The Amalekites] had the dubious distinction of being the first people of the world to attack and try to destroy God's newly formed covenant nation."[1]

6. The author implies that the perennial relationship of enmity between the Jews and the Agagites is mirrored in the personal relationship between Mordecai and Haman.[2]

7. Haman and King Xerxes are both enraged by the breach of respect. Both Haman and the king's advisers try to use their absolute power to punish and command respect for the larger representative group rather than just the individual they are angry with.

8. Haman appeals to King Xerxes' desire for power, both in terms of his subjects' obedience as well as his treasury that was depleted by war with Greece. Ten thousand talents was close to Xerxes' annual revenue.[3]

9. We see God's sovereignty working through providence in the casting of the lot. For God's people in Susa, the question of whether he was still working according to his covenant promises was a critical question—and a major theme of the entire book.

10. It's incredibly ironic that the edict for the Jews' destruction is sent out on the eve of Passover, the historic eve of God's deliverance of the Jews from the Egyptians.

11. Mordecai saved the life of King Xerxes, yet Haman is plotting against him. The Jews were living in relative peace, assimilated into Persian culture, yet were targeted for systematic destruction. Mordecai's trust in God's justice and goodness toward his people is being sorely tested.

12. Faith does not guarantee blessing. In fact, Jesus promised his disciples that following in his footsteps would bring difficulty (Mark 13:13; John 15:18–20; 1 Peter 2:20–21). Yet, his promise also stands that he will never leave us (Matt. 28:20).

NOTES

1. Jobes, 120.
2. See Jobes, 119–120.
3. See Jobes, 121.

SESSION 4 LEADER'S NOTES

Though none of us wants to invite difficulty into our lives, most of us would agree that character development happens most often when things are tough. This session can help you think about the effects of suffering in your own life and how you can encourage others in the midst of difficulties. Even though we might not embrace suffering and difficulty at the time, they are God's tools of transformation to make us the people he wants us to become.

1. Mordecai and the Jews tear their clothes, put on sackcloth and ashes, fast, weep, and wail. Esther tries to stop Mordecai from acting in such a way.
2. Esther does not have the freedom to approach the king anytime she wants, and his affection for her seems to have cooled recently.
3. Esther must decide whether to identify with her own people or try to hide herself in the inner sanctum of the Persian courts. She chooses to stand with her people.
4. Esther is instructing Mordecai rather than vice versa. This is a defining moment for Esther in which she assumes identity with and leadership for her people.
5. Mordecai recognizes God's judgment of his people through Haman, but also has hope that God will relent if his people rend their hearts and garments.
6. Esther 4:14: "And *who knows* but that you have come to royal position for such a time as this?"
   Joel 2:14: "*Who knows?* He may turn and relent."
   Esther came to understand that her only hope was found in being a child of God and turning to him for help, allowing herself to be his instrument of grace.
7. Esther is, in a sense, sounding the battle cry, committing herself to fight to the death for her people, aided and strengthened by their prayers and fasting.
8. Esther changes from being a weak, submissive character, taking all her orders from someone else, to someone who takes charge of her life for the higher goal of saving her people, even while it might mean the sacrifice of her own life for the cause.

9. Esther plays up to the king's desire for personal pleasure by asking him to a banquet, but the advantage she is seeking is mainly for the benefit of others, not just herself.

10. Esther shows, among other things, courage, wisdom, creativity, and patience in this section.

11. This should be something that is continually changing in all of our lives, not something that we look back on from months or even years ago. Consider these things carefully and prayerfully with the help of the Spirit himself.

12. It is helpful to think about specific situations in your own life. At the same time, none of us has the wisdom we would like to have to influence others in the right direction. Ultimately, we are best pointing others to Christ, as he will be the one to lead and guide each of us in a Godward direction.

SESSION 5 LEADER'S NOTES

Our understanding of the book of Esther is not complete if we don't look backward and forward in the fullness of God's story to get the big picture. The reversals for the characters in Esther are reflected in the bigger story of redemptive history—the extent to which we have disobeyed God, and the reversal he has brought about through Christ to give us the gift of new life. The good news of the gospel is integral to this great story of the Bible, although many people might miss it if they stick to a surface reading of it.

1. Haman's pride is rooted in his status gained by wealth, offspring, and the king's favor. Mordecai seems to be the only thing that irks him, refusing to bow down to him like everyone else.
2. Haman plans to hang Mordecai on a gallows that is as big as his own pride. He consistently takes advantage of his power for his own gain, even at the expense of human life. Haman's pride is again revealed the next morning, when he assumes he is the one the king wants to honor.
3. Everything changes as a result of the king's sleepless night. It is the turning point of the whole story. Mordecai receives the honor that was due him and Haman's downfall begins.
4. God is clearly directing the outcome of this story, even through something as mundane as a sleepless night.
5. Mordecai is paraded through the streets on the king's horse, in the king's robe, with Haman himself proclaiming the king's honor. Haman concluded just what would be the highest honor in his own eyes, as he imagined himself in Mordecai's place. The humiliation of Haman would be a wonder to behold!
6. Before the king's sleepless night, Haman could hardly be happier: he was reveling in both his pride and the destruction of Mordecai, the one man who filled him with rage. After the king's sleepless night, Haman rushes home filled with grief—he has been the instrument in honoring the man who filled him with rage, and his plans for the destruction of Mordecai are bound to cost him his own life, along with everything that was such a source of pride for a brief time.
7. At a point in time when God's people wondered if they would ever be in relationship with their God again, it is very significant that his favor still

rests with his people. His promises remain true even while his people live questionable lives in Persia.

8. God is always at work, even when he is not mentioned or seen, both in the big events that topple nations and the smallest details that cause a sleepless night. He rules over all people and all nations, not just the people of Israel, though he shows special favor to his own. From that, we can also say that God is faithful to his promises, even when the covenant agreement is broken on Israel's part. He is responsive to those who cry out to him for help, accomplishing his purposes even through weak faith.

9. Just as Israel was punished for its disobedience and sent out of the Promised Land, apart from the temple which represented the very presence of God, so Adam and Eve, representing all humanity, were banished from the garden of Eden, with all of its promise and close relationship with God himself. Sin has tainted everything since, including our nature, our thinking, our choices, and our world. No longer could a stained humanity stand before a perfect God. Death entered into the world with brutal force and terrifying consequences.

10. Nothing can separate God's people from the love of God. Jesus, the one who stands as judge, is the very one who gave his life to save us. He promises to be with us, no matter how great the enemy or hardship. Thanks be to God!

11. This is a good time to celebrate the joys and even sorrows God has brought you through, either individually or corporately. Take time to think, listen, and remember, perhaps seeing some things for the first time through God-shaped lenses.

SESSION 6 LEADER'S NOTES

1. "In the king's rhetoric, the two words 'petition' and 'request' refer to the one and the same desire of Esther. Her reply is rhetorically structured exactly as was his question: 'Grant me my life—this is my petition. And spare my people—this is my request.' By framing her response using the king's rhetoric, Esther is saying that her life and the life of her people are one and the same. Her destiny is one with her people."[1]

2. The edict against the Jews was actually issued in King Xerxes' name. Esther has to be careful not to put any blame on him and jeopardize her petition.

3. "Esther's words send Xerxes into an enraged quandary that drives him out of the banquet room and into the garden. In his commentary, M. Fox reads the questions circulating in Xerxes' mind: 'Can he punish Haman for a plot he himself approved? If he does so, won't he have to admit his own role in the fiasco [and lose face]? Moreover, he has issued an irrevocable law; how then can he rescind it?' "[2]

4. (1) Instead of the king honoring Haman, he has him sentenced to death as a traitor; (2) Mordecai is now being honored in place of Haman; (3) Zeresh, Haman's wife, recognized that her husband is doomed since he has gone against the Jews; (4) Haman's pride, position, wealth, status in the community, and everything else are all gone.

5. Haman has used his absolute power for nothing but selfish and evil purposes, which hasn't gained him any friends. His puffed-up pride was dependent on the king's good opinion—having lost that, Haman has nothing to stand on. Ultimately, Haman pursued a path that was against God's people, which was doomed to eventual but inevitable failure. There were many details beyond Haman's control, yet he chose a path that in the end can only result in destruction.

6. King Xerxes may have been angry about Haman's threat to Esther and her people, but used the convenient excuse of Haman's proximity to Esther as a good reason to have him punished. The fact that the king's fury subsides once Haman is executed suggests that he was more concerned about the threat to his queen than to her people. When Harbona points out that Haman had a gallows built for Mordecai, it also suggests that Haman

could be a traitor—planning on killing the very man who saved the king. In Queen Esther and Mordecai's eyes, Haman was guilty not only of being an enemy of the Jews but specifically threatening their own lives as well. God knew Haman's heart best of all. In addition to being an enemy of God's people, Haman could be found guilty of greed, pride, abuse of power, and a host of other evils.

7. "Driven by uncontrollable pride and arrogance, Haman had plotted to slaughter the Jewish people because his lust for power over others could not be satisfied as long as Mordecai the Jew refused to bow to him. Given full rein, pride, like greed and lust, is insatiable.... His plan to take revenge on one man by annihilating his entire race was an evil of demonic proportions, regardless of who those people were.... His sudden and unpreventable destruction was the just reward of such an evil mind."[3]

8. "Human evil, wherever it occurs and for whatever motivation, always sets itself against God, because God is the definition of goodness and righteousness. Divine justice inevitably and inextricably means the destruction of evil. The author of Esther shows that evil is personal. It is not some ethereal substance 'out there'; evil does not exist apart from beings who are evil. Therefore, in order to deliver the Jewish people from annihilation as God promised in his covenant with them, God necessarily had to destroy the evil that threatened their existence. In this case that evil came in the person of Haman. Mercy on Haman would have been inconsistent with God's covenant."[4]

9. "Esther's role as queen of the Jews in the story makes it inappropriate to use exemplary exegesis as the key to understanding this book. Esther is not portrayed as the ideal woman of God living out her relationship with the Lord as a direct example for women today. Her role as the Jewish queen of Persia in a specific stage of redemptive history and biblical theology means that no other woman can or should try to emulate directly her character or behavior, just as no Christian man today would emulate David when he killed two hundred Philistines for their foreskins as the bride price for Saul's daughter (1 Sam. 18:24–30)."[5] The true example of Esther we must follow is, at every decision point, to identify ourselves with the people of God in Christ.

10. Keep in mind not only the right actions and attitudes that should characterize our lives as Christians, but also the grace and forgiveness that is found through the new life we receive through Christ.
11. Of course there is a difference between dealing with sin in our daily lives and being wholeheartedly aligned with an evil lifestyle. But there is great danger in only thinking of "other people out there" as ones who do wrong and not taking a careful look at the sin in our own lives.

NOTES

1. See Jobes, 164.
2. Quoted in Jobes, 165.
3. Jobes, 171–172.
4. Jobes, 172.
5. Jobes, 169.

SESSION 7 LEADER'S NOTES

1. The king had Esther's enemy killed and gave her his estate, but Esther's petition was actually to save her life and the life of her people. The king eased his own anger at Haman's actions but did nothing toward actually saving the Jews from their predicament.

2. In the king's own words (8:8), "No document written in the king's name and sealed with his ring can be revoked." Perhaps this was so because it would undermine a king's authority, or perhaps, as pointed out in the "Going Deeper" quote following question 2, it is just a literary device used by the author of Esther. In either case, Esther and Mordecai came up with a counter-decree that gave the Jews the power to defend themselves, essentially creating a civil war in Persia, but not overruling the original decree.

3. The orders look virtually identical, although the TNIV translation gives the impression that the Jews will only act defensively toward those who would harm them. The interpretation might depend on the view of the translator as to how ethical holy war is. "The extent of the parity between Haman's decree of death and Mordecai's counter-decree is obscured by the NIV translation.... In [the majority] reading of the Hebrew text, the Jews were given exactly the same terms of destruction that had been pronounced against them, their women, and their children."[1]

4. The counter-decree marks a great victory for the Jewish people, even before it is carried out. Apparently their God is still working on their behalf and is supreme over the nations. Instead of being wiped off the face of the earth, the Jews gain supremacy over their enemies. Queen Esther can truly be recognized as an honorable Jewish, as well as Persian, queen who used her influence on behalf of her people.

5. The king's signet ring given to Haman in 3:10 is given to Mordecai in 8:2.

   Haman's decree in 3:12 is countered by Mordecai's decree in 8:9–10.

   Orders to destroy the Jews in 3:13 are reversed by giving the Jews the right to assemble and protect themselves in 8:11.

   In 3:14, the people of Persia prepare to kill the Jews, but in 8:13 the Jews prepare to avenge themselves on the people.

   The city of Susa is bewildered in 3:15, but rejoices in 8:14, 15b.

Mordecai dresses in sackcloth in 4:1 but is clothed royally in 8:15a.

6. This is troublesome for many people, causing some to create a great divide between the message, and even the God, of the Old Testament and New Testament. Hopefully the remainder of this session will be helpful in thinking this through. God has not changed over time, and there is a continuity between the Old and New Testament. But it is important to recognize in which period of redemptive history Esther is living. Because we live on this side of the cross of Christ, who has destroyed our enemy once and for all, we need to have a different approach toward our enemies than Esther and the Jews of her time. Holy war does not have a one-to-one correspondence or application to us in the redemptive period we live in because of the death and resurrection of Jesus Christ.

7. Holy war was declared on the Anakites because of their complete and utter wickedness.

8. As God's people, the Jews were used as his instruments of judgment on the Anakites. The Deuteronomy passage stresses that it had nothing to do with the Jews' righteousness — they were a stiff-necked people.

9. The consequences of sin in the garden of Eden were death and judgment. No one was found worthy of God, so he came himself in the flesh, through his Son Jesus Christ, to destroy the enemy by taking on all the punishment himself. Faith in Jesus enables us to stand before God in Christ's righteousness, pure and faultless, reversing the judgment that was in store for us. "Consequently, just as one trespass resulted in condemnation for all people, so also one righteous act resulted in justification and life for all" (Rom. 5:18).

10. Holy war has always been about defeating the enemy, Satan. Before Christ, that was manifested physically in nations that would destroy God's people. God used his people as a means to judge other wicked nations. Since Christ has defeated Satan once and for all, the skirmishes that remain are against sins that we still struggle with. Christ leveled the field by taking on God's punishment of *our* sin. Our job now is to show that love to all who will receive it, battling sin by telling others of the forgiveness we have in Christ.

11. God has equipped us to fight against sin and the devil's schemes with the spiritual armor described in Ephesians 6:10 – 18. The battle happens in

the details of everyday life as we fight the attitudes, words, and actions that cause us to sin in our relationships and daily activities. There is great honor and joy in living pleasing lives before God, and extending God's love to those around us. Think about this in the practical outworking of your faith, not just some ethereal spirituality. God works in the details!

NOTE

1. Jobes, 180.

SESSION 8 LEADER'S NOTES

1. The structuring of reversals in the book leads the reader to be assured of the Jews' victory. What is more, the God of creation, true to his covenant with his people, is orchestrating events such that the Jews cannot lose.

    "Because Mordecai's decree expressed God's ancient decree of survival for his people and the destruction of their enemies, it was a done deal before the day dawned. The decree in effect guaranteed the outcome. The author is showing it is God's decree, his word, that assures the survival of his people; the rest is just detail. But it is important detail, because it shows that God's word is truly effective in the outworking of human history. God is capable of doing exactly what he says he will do, even centuries after he says it. This episode highlights the powerful efficacy of God's word as it is actualized in history through flawed, and even evil, people."[1]

2. The Jews killed and destroyed their enemies, doing what they pleased to those who hated them. However, they did not lay hands on any of the plunder, even though the king's edict would have allowed them to do so. This was consistent with the concept of holy war for the Jews.

3. Esther requests that the Jews continue the destruction of their enemies for one more day in the city of Susa, and that the sons of Haman be hanged for public viewing. Many believe Esther might be going overboard here. Holy war required that none of Haman's sons be allowed to live, so that his line would not rise up against God's people again in the future. See the quote following question 3.

4. As mentioned in question 1, God's hand guarantees the outcome of events, so in that sense we see his behind-the-scenes activity. However, unlike miracles such as the crossing of the Red Sea, we do not see the direct intervention of God. It is Mordecai and Esther who convince the king to send out a second decree. It is the Jews who arm themselves and kill their enemies. They took responsibility for the circumstances, even while God providentially assured their victory.

5. God's involvement in the first victory against the Amalekites is much more direct and miraculous than in Esther, where we see his providence at work. His power is demonstrated through the holding up of Moses' staff — anytime it is lowered, the battle turns against the Israelites. However, in both

instances, God is faithful in bringing victory to the people with whom he has made a covenant.

6. Without Mordecai's written record and instruction to celebrate this day throughout all generations, the thirteenth of Adar may have been a moment in history remembered for a generation and then forgotten over time. But the institution of Purim as a holiday on par with those God established in Moses' time makes it a celebration of God's faithfulness, even though he is never once mentioned in the book of Esther. In Exodus (17:14), God commands that records be written so that the incident is never forgotten; again, God's role is explicit there, but in Esther it's Mordecai's idea to send out letters.

7. God is faithful to the covenant with his people, even when they are unfaithful. He demonstrates his continuing love for his people through the preservation of a remnant throughout history, even when the nation of Israel that he established has been conquered and dispersed.

8. "Because of [Jesus'] resurrection, Christians can face death with the assurance that we ourselves will not be defeated by the grave but will triumph over it against all human expectation. The deliverance of the Jews in Persia foreshadows the redemption of those from all nations who enter into God's covenant through Jesus the Messiah."[2]

9. Miracles certainly attest to the power of God and have been used by him dramatically in unbelieving generations. But there have been many who saw miracles and returned for more miracles, not for the spiritual truth behind them (for example, John 6:26). Jesus told Thomas, "Blessed are those who have not seen and yet have believed" (John 20:29). Faith in any generation requires trusting the God we cannot see with our eyes, but who is always at work anyway.

10. Every Sunday, and Easter in particular, is a celebration of Jesus' resurrection, the final proof that God has destroyed the enemy of his people and death itself. Celebration is an important way of remembering God's faithfulness and teaching it to the next generation. Judges 2:10–11 points out the dangers of not doing so: "After that whole generation had been gathered to their ancestors, another generation grew up who knew neither the LORD nor what he had done for Israel. Then the Israelites did evil in the eyes of the LORD and served the Baals." People are prone to wander

when they do not "continue to work out [their] salvation with fear and trembling" (Phil. 2:12).

11. Just as all the Jews, not only ordained leaders, had to take responsibility in light of the circumstances during Esther's time, the laity of the church are responsible today to be Jesus' hands and feet. In fact, as the priesthood of believers, all Christians are especially equipped by the Holy Spirit and have been given new life by God as "God's handiwork, created in Christ Jesus to do good works, which God prepared in advance for us to do" (Eph. 2:10). In this way "the whole body, joined and held together by every supporting ligament, grows and builds itself up in love, as each part does its work" (Eph. 4:16).

12. "In our society women and men receive the same education in the classroom, fill the same positions in the workplace, and worship side by side in the church. Scripture affirms that both women and men bear the image of God (Gen. 1:27) and have equal standing in Christ (Gal. 3:28). The relationship of men and women in community outside the family should work for the glory of God and the fulfillment of his redemptive purposes.... The story of how Esther and Mordecai share responsibility in a mutually dependent way is a story that dignifies the role of the laity. It affords the church the opportunity to reflect on the part the laity have to play in the larger picture of life and redemptive history."[3]

NOTES

1. Jobes, 203.
2. Jobes, 220.
3. Jobes, 229–230.

The NIV Application Commentary

Esther

Karen H. Jobes

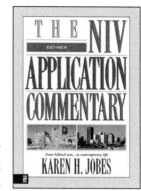

Most Bible commentaries take us on a one-way trip from our world to the world of the Bible. But they leave us there, assuming that we can somehow make the return journey on our own. In other words, they focus on the original meaning of the passage but don't discuss its contemporary application. The information they offer is valuable — but the job is only half done!

The NIV Application Commentary helps us with both halves of the interpretive task. This new and unique series shows readers how to bring an ancient message into a modern context. It explains not only what the Bible meant but also how it can speak powerfully today.

This volume on the Old Testament book of Esther unpacks the intriguing narrative of a Jewish woman and her cousin, Mordecai, who stayed behind in Persia following the exile — and how they were instrumental in saving God's people in that place. With no mention of God anywhere in the book of Esther, it nonetheless illustrates his sovereignty over all things and his faithfulness to his covenant promises.

The story of Esther is perfect guidance for us when we find ourselves in a situation where right and wrong are not so clearly defined and every choice we have seems to be a troubling mixture of good and bad.

Hardcover, Jacketed: 978-0-310-20672-9

Pick up a copy today at your favorite bookstore!

Share Your Thoughts

With the Author: Your comments will be forwarded to the author when you send them to *zauthor@zondervan.com*.

With Zondervan: Submit your review of this book by writing to *zreview@zondervan.com*.

Free Online Resources at
www.zondervan.com/hello

 Zondervan AuthorTracker: Be notified whenever your favorite authors publish new books, go on tour, or post an update about what's happening in their lives.

 Daily Bible Verses and Devotions: Enrich your life with daily Bible verses or devotions that help you start every morning focused on God.

 Free Email Publications: Sign up for newsletters on fiction, Christian living, church ministry, parenting, and more.

 Zondervan Bible Search: Find and compare Bible passages in a variety of translations at www.zondervanbiblesearch.com.

 Other Benefits: Register yourself to receive online benefits like coupons and special offers, or to participate in research.